CW01395343

Published by Evans Brothers Limited
2A Portman Mansions
Chiltern Street
London W1M 1LE

First published in Great Britain in 1982 by
Hamish Hamilton Children's Books

© The Archon Press 1982

Reprinted 1992

Originated by David Cook and Associates

Printed in Belgium

ISBN 0 237 60237 7

Jungles

Henry Pluckrose
consultant editor

Illustrated by
Richard Orr

small
WORLD

Evans Brothers Limited

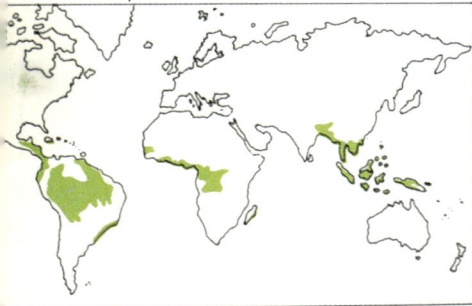

Rain forests

A jungle is a kind of forest; it is often called a 'rain forest'.

Rain forests are found in parts of the world which are hot and rainy.

The trees grow very tall and block out the light.

There is no wind inside the forest and everything is quiet and still.

Nearly everything in a rain forest is green. Colourful flowers are only found near rivers or clearings.

A section of a rain forest

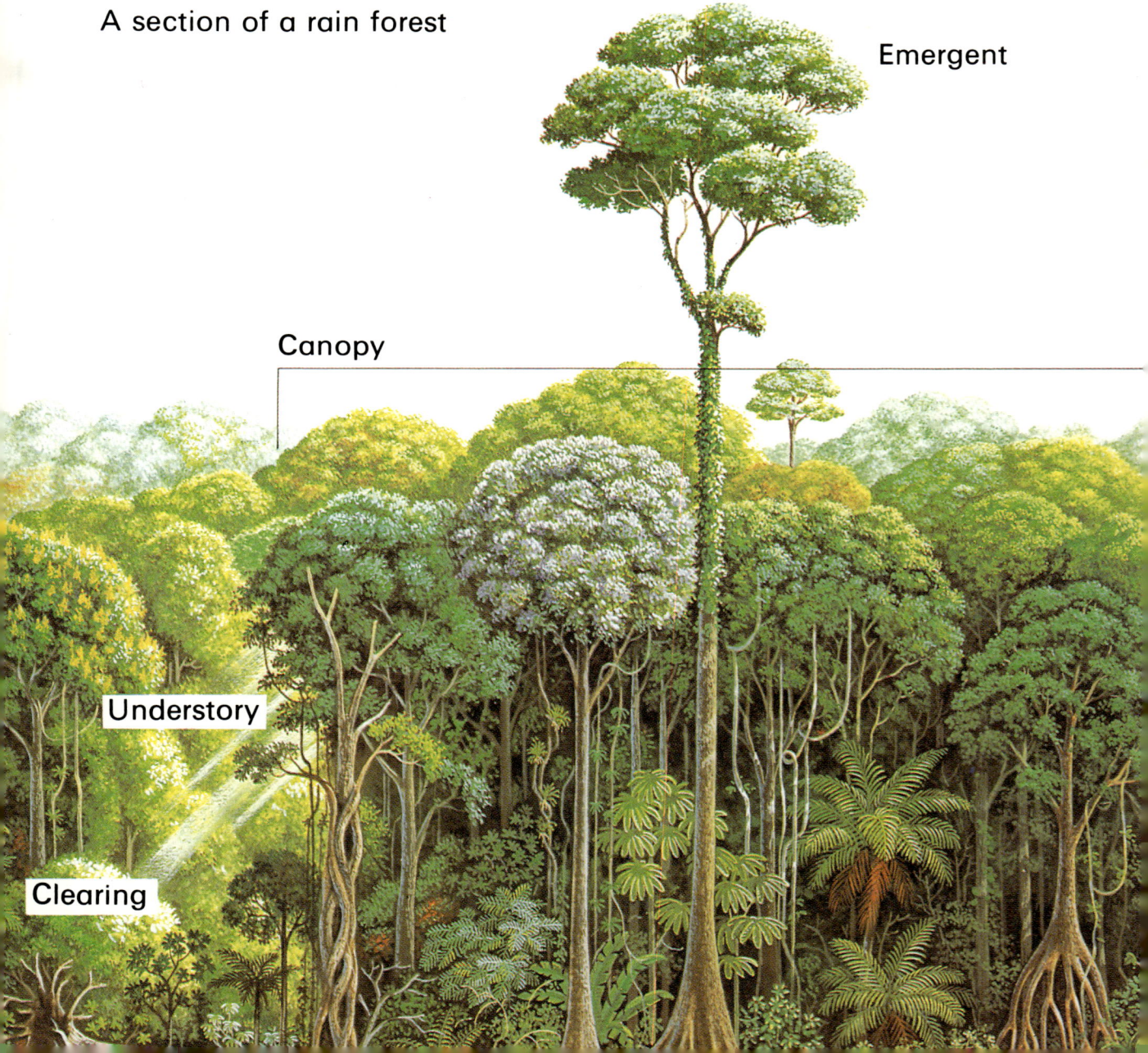

Emergent

Canopy

Understory

Clearing

In the forest a few trees grow up to a height of 70 metres.

They are called emergents.

Many more trees are between 30 and 70 metres tall. Their leaves form a kind of roof called the canopy.

Another layer of trees and plants grows beneath the canopy. This is called the understory.

Because there are so many trees, very little light gets through to the forest floor. Hardly anything grows there.

Bromeliad

Bromeliad

Elkhorn fern

Lichen

Plants need light to live, and they reach it
by growing up the trunks and branches
of trees. These include orchids, ferns,
bromeliads, mosses and lichens.
Vines and creepers also climb the trees.
They only produce leaves when they
find enough light.

Pink orchid

Purple orchid

Orange orchid

Moss

Cockatoo

Grey parrot

A huge variety of animals live in
rain forests.
Parrots and toucans have strong beaks to
crack nuts and seeds and tear fruit.
Humming birds use their long tongues to
sip the nectar from flowers.

Toucan

Violet saber-wing
hummingbird

Gold and blue
macaw

Ruby-throated
hummingbird

Sword-billed
hummingbird

There are many different kinds of bat.
Most bats eat insects and some eat fruit.
But the vampire bat (right) lives on the
blood it sucks from living animals.
Another bat (below left) sips nectar like
a humming bird.
The fishing bat (below right) fishes in the
rivers for its food.

Most animals in the forest are good climbers. Here are some climbing animals from Indonesia.

The orang-utan (1) is heavy and climbs very carefully.
The gibbon (2) swings from branch to branch using only its arms.
Macaques (3) langurs (4) and tarsiers (5) are all leapers, using hand and foot.
The slow loris (6) moves deliberately from handhold to handhold.
The palm squirrel (7) and the jungle cat (8) use their claws for climbing.

The animals shown in the box can glide from tree to tree. Some can travel over 75 metres in this way.

Draco

Flying squirrel

Colugo

Flying frog

Flying snake

Tree iguana

The upper canopy is the home of many strange animals. They are small because the branches cannot support the weight of large animals.
Most eat leaves, fruit and plants, although some hunt other animals.
The largest animals found in the canopy are monkey-eating eagles.

A South American forest canopy
1. Monkey-eating eagle
2. Squirrel monkeys
3. Opossum
4. Sloth
5. Tree snake
6. Macaws
7. Howler monkeys
8. Morpho butterfly
9. Caterpillar
10. Praying mantis
11. Thorn bug

The understory is a shady tangle of smaller tree branches, vines and creepers. Some animals just travel through it, but for others it is home.

A huge variety of insects live here and they provide food for numerous bats and birds. This picture shows the understory in a South American forest.

Wrinkle-faced bats (1) roost during the day. A climbing anteater (2) feasts on an ants' nest (3). A chestnut woodpecker (4) searches for grubs in a dead tree.
You can also see:
Leaf grasshoppers (6, 7)
Giant stick insect (8)
Red-beaked wasp (9)
Shoemaker butterfly (10)
Noctuid moth (11)
Notodontid moth (12)

The forest is covered with dead leaves which quickly decay and become part of the soil. They enrich the soil and so help to feed the trees.

Many small animals live here, such as millipedes, mites, slugs, worms, beetles and snails.

An African forest floor
1. Millipede
2. Flatworm
3. Centipede
4. Lantern fly
5. Leech
6. Goliath beetle
7. Velvet worm
8. Phoebus butterflies
9. Horned frog

A lot of these creatures are eaten
by the many frogs and toads which live
on the forest floor.
Leeches lie in wait for any passing
animal. They attach themselves to its
skin and suck its blood.
Butterflies often gather in large numbers.

The jaguar is the
largest of the hunters.
It can swim well,
hunt on the ground
and climb.

Larger animals live mainly
in clearings or near rivers.
The capybara lives by the rivers of
South American rain forests. It rushes into
the water if it is attacked by
people or hunting animals.

Capybaras and young

The okapi lives in Africa.
It has white markings on its body, which
make it difficult to see in the shade
of the forest.

The leopard is the
largest common
hunter in the
forests of Africa
and Asia.

The river is important to many animals in the forest. In this picture of a South American river you can see a tapir, a jaguar, some capybara and some scarlet ibises.
None of these animals stray far from the water.

But the butterfly, the rhinoceros beetle, the humming bird and the squirrel monkey all live in the forest. They are usually difficult to see from the ground. This picture helps you see them clearly.

People have also made their homes in the jungle. But nowadays there are only a few tribes left.

Amazon Indians dip their arrows in poison to kill their prey more swiftly.
The poison is made from the skins of these little frogs.

Fruits, plants and even insects are an important part of forest-dwellers' food. They grow some crops themselves. They plant them in the ashes of trees they have burned down. The ashes make the soil more fertile. A few seasons later they make new clearings.

An Amazon Indian settlement.

Many forests have now been cut down for timber. In some places, crops such as bananas, pineapples, cocoa and pepper have been planted where there once were trees. But fewer and fewer people follow the traditional way of life and many animals and plants have disappeared.

Index